THE STORY OF SPACE

SATELLITES

Steve Parker

A⁺

Published by Smart Apple Media, an imprint of Black Rabbit Books
P.O. Box 3263, Mankato, Minnesota 56002
www.blackrabbitbooks.com

Produced by David West 🏃 Children's Books
6 Princeton Court, 55 Felsham Road, London SW15 1AZ

Designed by Gary Jeffrey

Cataloging-in-Publication Data is available from the Library of Congress.
ISBN 978-1-62588-079-6

CSPIA compliance information: DWCB14FCP
011014

9 8 7 6 5 4 3 2 1

All images courtesy of NASA except: p6b, Staffan Vilcans; p10l, andrzejolchawa; p11tl, Cliff,
p11tr, Klaus Därr, p11b, USAF (Los Angeles AFB); p12tl, Lockheed-Martin, p12br, DOD;
p13m, United States Air Force photo by Airman 1st Class Mike Meares, p13b, ESA; p14l,
p15tr, USGS/NASA; p15tl, NOAA Coastal Services Center Hawaii Land Cover Analysis
project, p15b, National Reconnaissance Office; p16-17 all, NOAA; p18bl, NASA Scientific
Visualization Studio; p19r, JAXA; p20mr, NASA Marshall Space Flight Center; p22tl, NASA,
ESA, HEIC, and The Hubble Heritage Team (STScI/AURA, p22m, CREDIT FOR HUBBLE
IMAGE: NASA, ESA, N. Smith (University of California, Berkeley), and The Hubble Heritage
Team STScI/AURA, p22b, University of California, Santa Cruz; R. Bouwens, Leiden University;
and the HUDF09 Team; p23t, Hubble Space Telescope Comet Team and NASA, p23b,
NASA, ESA and Hubble; p24bl, Image Science and Analysis Laboratory, NASA-Johnson
Space Center, p24br, NASA/CXC/CfA/P. Slane et al; p25tl, NASA, ESA, The Hubble Heritage
Team STScI-AURA, p25t, HST/NASA/ESA, p25m, NASA/JPL-Caltech/Univ.of Ariz; p26ml,
Pline; p27m, Jakub Halun, p27ml, US Navy photo, p27mr, NASA Orbital Debris Program
Office, p27b, Jwmissel; p29t, DARPA/Boeing

CONTENTS

By some distance the most important scientific satellite ever put into orbit, the Hubble Space Telescope enabled astronomers to view stars and galaxies in previously unimagined detail. Its optics and systems have been continually upgraded by Shuttle missions. Hubble has even enabled astronomers to begin divining the origins of the Universe.

INTRODUCTION

In space, a satellite is an object locked in orbit, following its curved path around a more massive object. It was long understood that the Moon orbited the Earth in this way. A method for placing artificial satellites in orbit around Earth was first suggested in 1903.

Fifty years passed until the technology was ready. Then beeping *Sputnik 1*, speeding up to 17,000 miles (25,000 km) per hour, circled the globe. More than 3,000 satellites from 50 different countries have since been placed in orbit—forever changing the way we see the world, communicate, and view the cosmos.

A Boeing Delta IV heavy lift vehicle, or "rocket," blasts a US GOES weather satellite on its journey into orbit. The Delta is one of several orbital launchers used by the 10 or so spacefaring nations. An average of 120 satellites are launched every year.

THE SPUTNIK SHOCK

In 1955 the US announced it would launch an artificial satellite during an upcoming series of international Earth science experiments. Meanwhile the USSR (Soviet Union), its superpower rival, was working on a secret project of its own.

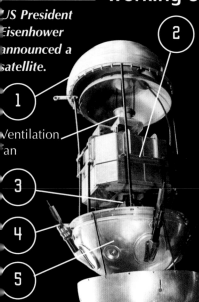

US President Eisenhower announced a satellite.

1

Ventilation fan

3

4

5

1

THE SOVIETS GEAR UP

2

The original Soviet plan for an ambitious orbiting laboratory had quickly proved impossible. In 1957 the project was scaled down to a simple probe that would transmit temperature and pressure data. It was christened *Sputnik* ("Companion"). Fastracked by Soviet space genius Sergey Korolyov, it would be launched atop his new R-7 missile design.

In eight months it was ready. On October 4, at 10:28 pm Moscow time, the rocket launched and successfully placed *Sputnik 1* into orbit. After a tense 90 minutes, Soviet ground stations received a stream of beeps—a signal that the world had just changed.

A Soviet engineer prepares Sputnik 1 *for its flight.*

INSIDE SPUTNIK 1

1. **OUTER CASING** Spherical to reduce atmospheric drag
2. **INSTRUMENT CASING** Two transmitters and two batteries
3. **SENSORS** For measuring temperature and pressure in space
4. **ANTENNA MOUNT**
5. **INNER CASING** Pressurized to protect instruments

Sputnik 1 took the US completely by surprise. The sudden Soviet domination of space caused both scientific interest and public fear, as the Americans worked desperately to get into orbit.

In 1957 the Soviet R-7 rocket was the only launch system in the world capable of lofting a Sputnik-sized payload into orbit.

Sputnik 1's success "put a glow" on the face of Soviet Premier Khrushchev. It also appeared to back up his claims of Soviet missile superiority.

TOO LITTLE TOO QUICKLY

US President Eisenhower insisted his nation was on target for December launch. Then the Soviets successfully launched a dog into orbit. The team developing the US Vanguard rocket and its diminutive TV3 satellite—the size of a grapefruit—were rushed into a launch, with explosively disastrous results. US dignity was in tatters.

Watched by the world's press, a US Navy Vanguard TV rocket exploded on the launch pad on December 6,1957.

VON BRAUN'S BOYS

Luckily, a second project headed by US-German rocket pioneer Wernher von Braun was already under way. Using a tried-and-tested adaptation of his Redstone missile, von Braun's team designed an instrument-bearing nose cone, satellite *Explorer 1*, fitted to a baby rocket casing. A second-stage ring of small rockets fired in sequence to separate and propel *Explorer 1* into orbit. The design worked better than expected, throwing *Explorer 1* three times farther than *Sputnik 1*'s 550 miles (900 km). The US was in the space race.

VANGUARD TV3

Solar cells

Antenna

Vanguard's tiny satellite (left) was mangled.

Turnstile antenna wire

EXPLORER 1

Nose cone

A Redstone rocket rises on a column of flame, lifting Explorer 1 *into the night sky on January 31, 1958.*

RADIATION belts **detected** by *EXPLORER 1* are **named** after its **instrument-maker,** James **VAN ALLEN**.

A triumphant von Braun (far right) and his team hold aloft a model of the first US satellite in orbit.

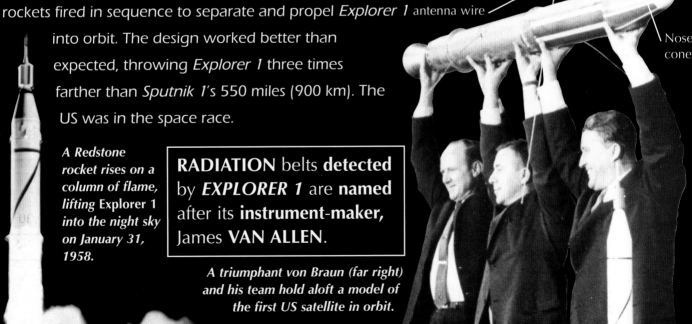

THE FIRST SATELLITES

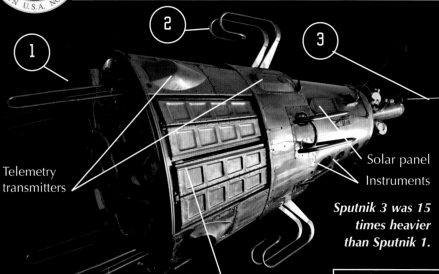

Telemetry transmitters

Solar panel
Instruments

Sputnik 3 was 15 times heavier than Sputnik 1.

T**he "Sputnik Crisis" led US President Eisenhower to sign the National Aeronautics and Space Act in 1958, creating NASA. Meanwhile the Soviets completed their orbiting laboratory idea, as *Sputnik 3*.**

SPUTNIK 3

1. **COMMAND RADIO LINK**
2. **TELEMETRY ANTENNA** Transmits data from scientific instruments using high speed radio wavelengths
3. **RADIO BEACON** Transmits data from scientific instruments using telegraphic signals
4. **COOLING BLINDS** Open or close for temperature control

LABS AND REFLECTORS

Sputnik 3 was the first fully equipped geophysical probe (although it failed to map the Van Allen Belts when its tape recorder broke). Having won the satellite race, the Soviets turned their attention to secretly developing their powerful rockets for human spaceflight.

Meanwhile the US developed satellite potential. The first radio broadcast from space was a tape of President Eisenhower, beamed to the world at Christmas, 1958. In 1959 spy satellite *Discoverer 13* took the first space pictures to be returned to Earth. *Project Echo,* a mylar balloon, was inflated in orbit to reflect radio signals back to Earth.

NASA's **Project Echo** *remains the largest single satellite ever orbited.*

Solar cells

TV camera

TIROS 1, *an early Low Earth Orbit weather satellite, took the first-ever TV footage of Earth from space. Its infrared camera ushered in the era of Earth remote sensing.*

Using their solar panels for energy, Telstar satellites were the first to amplify the signals they received before relaying them back to Earth.

The Telstars relayed telephone, fax, data, and live and taped television via enormous horn-shaped ground receivers. These rotated to track a signal that was impossibly weak by today's standards.

TRAILBLAZERS

Networks of radio telescope tracking stations and ships spread across Earth. The goal was global communications coverage. As early as 1945, science fiction writer Arthur C. Clarke had promoted the idea of geostationary Earth orbit, GEO—the height where a satellite's speed matched the rotation of Earth. At 22,236 miles (35,786 km) high, moving at 1,070 miles (1,670 km) per hour, it would "hover" over one spot all day and night.

GEO was pioneered by NASA with the *Syncom* relay satellites. Weather satellites like *Nimbus* orbited closer to Earth, around the Poles, crossing the Equator at a set time (Sun-synchronous) to ensure the same daily Sun angle.

SYNCOM 3

① 1

① 1

② 2

③ 3

④ 4

*From 1964, NASA's large **Nimbus** meteorological satellites revolutionized weather prediction. They enabled three- to five-day forecasts for the first time.*

NIMBUS   Solar panel

Horizon scanner

Infrared radiometers

Infrared spectrometers

SYNCOM 3

1. **ANTENNA**
2. **SOLAR PANELS**
3. **KICK MOTOR** To boost satellite up from Low Earth Orbit to Medium Earth Orbit
4. **SOLAR SENSOR**

Syncom 3, launched in 1964, was the first satellite placed in geostationary orbit—mainly to relay TV coverage of the 1964 Summer Olympics from Tokyo to the US and Europe.

There are **currently** over **400** active **GEOSTATIONARY satellites.** Any **country** is **ALLOWED** to **ask** for a **SLOT.**

Communications satellites, or comsats, were regarded as so important that an international organization, Intelsat, was set up solely to organize their geostationary orbits (GEOs).

Modern comsats use antennae to receive radio, TV, telephone, and internet signals, and bounce them back to Earth via transmitters.

Transmitter

Launched in 1974, NASA's ATS-6 comsat was the first three-axis stabilized geostationary satellite

ZONING IN

Antennae

Solar panels

Intelsat's first satellite, *Early Bird* (based on *Syncom 3*), gained orbit in 1965. Early comsats were generally drum-like, coated in photovoltaic (solar) cells, and were stabilized by spinning themselves, like gyroscopes. NASA led the way once again with the *Applications Technology Satellite-6* (ATS-6) which used small thrusters and momentum wheels for positional control. Three-axis (3D) stabilization meant accurate pointing was possible. *ATS-6* could track satellites below it, allowing NASA to build an orbiting communications network. *ATS-6* also pioneered satellite TV beamed direct to homes.

NASA uses Tracking and Data Relay Satellites (TDRS) across its Space Network to send commands to spacecraft, receive scientific data from satellites, and monitor astronaut health.

NASA TDRS-L

Crosslink antenna

Antenna

Down link

INTELSAT 6

Orbiter's robot arm

Comsats sometimes experience problems getting geostationary. In 1992 three Shuttle astronauts had to manhandle a marooned Intelsat onto a new booster after robot arm tools failed to secure it

Replacement booster rocket

Orbiter's payload bay

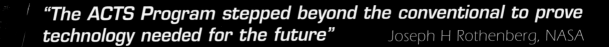

Solar array

The Iridium satellite phone network uses a constellation of 66 satellites that circle the Poles at a Low Earth Orbit of 485 miles (780 km). Equipped with an Iridium-capable phone, a person can be contacted anywhere on Earth at any time, no matter how remote.

Gateway antenna

SATELLITE PHONE HANDSETS

Inmarsat Iridium Thuraya

MOTOROLA
IRIDIUM SATELLITE

Main mission antenna Crosslink antenna

DIGI COMMS

Satellite telephones are vital for the military, shipping, and disaster agencies. Important international money transactions are via satellite. Portable receiver/transmitter dishes enable TV images from any major news story around the globe to appear almost immediately.

The digital revolution that allowed these wonders began in 1992 when NASA launched the *Advanced Communications Technology Satellite* (*ACTS*). Just like a high-speed digital switchboard, *ACTS* could do the work of many satellites at once, preventing the geostationary orbit from overcrowding.

Satellite dishes allow access to the modern world from almost inaccessible places.

NASA let **companies** use *ACTS* as a **TESTBED,** leading to the **powerful COMMUNICATIONS SATELLITES** we have **TODAY.**

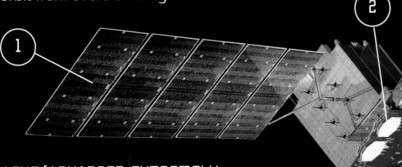

AEHF (ADVANCED EXTREMELY HIGH FREQUENCY) COMSAT

1. **SOLAR ARRAY**
2. **SPOT BEAM ANTENNA**
3. **CROSSLINK ANTENNA** Satellite link up between *AEHF* and *MILSTAR* satellites
4. **HIGH RESOLUTION ANTENNA** Operates even when jamming is attempted

AEHF is a recent US Air Force comsat. Each AEHF unit provides greater capacity than all five of the older MILSTAR comsats combined.

NAVIGATION

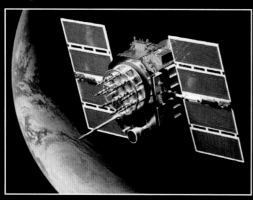

T he Global Positioning System (GPS), a worldwide satellite navigation network, was developed from the US need to coordinate nuclear strikes in the event of World War III.

The first GPS satellite, Navstar 1, was launched in 1978. Its solar arrays charged batteries for use in Earth's shadow.

TRIANGULATED

GPS satellites circle Earth twice a day, transmitting a regular signal containing a time and location code. A GPS receiver on the ground registers how long the signal took to arrive and calculates the distance to the satellite. Using signals from three satellites, the receiver triangulates its position on a ground map. Using a fourth signal, it can also calculate the receiver's altitude.

GPS is accurate to within 25 feet (7.8 meters). Its US *Navstar* satellite systems cost billions to set up, yet its use is free.

The current GPS constellation of 24 Medium Earth Orbit satellites are at 15° to the Equator. This means at any location, at least four satellites are always 15° above the horizon.

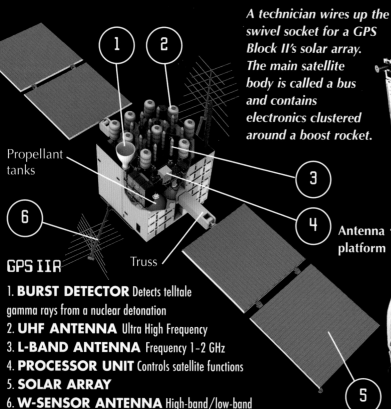

A technician wires up the swivel socket for a GPS Block II's solar array. The main satellite body is called a bus and contains electronics clustered around a boost rocket.

Propellant tanks

Antenna platform

Truss

Socket on bus

GPS IIR

1. **BURST DETECTOR** Detects telltale gamma rays from a nuclear detonation
2. **UHF ANTENNA** Ultra High Frequency
3. **L-BAND ANTENNA** Frequency 1–2 GHz
4. **PROCESSOR UNIT** Controls satellite functions
5. **SOLAR ARRAY**
6. **W-SENSOR ANTENNA** High-band/low-band

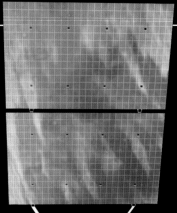

The next generation of US Navstars, GPS Block III, features boosted signal strength. They share a civilian signal band, L1, with other GP systems. They will operate for 15 years.

Dedicated handheld GPS navigation devices are carried by hikers, cyclists, trekkers, and many others to navigate unfamiliar territory.

System bus

W-sensor

Antennae

APPLICATIONS

The first widespread civilian use of GPS was for in-vehicle navigation. Now most smartphones are GPS-capable—useful if you happen to lose your phone! Emergency beacons on ships and aircraft have GPS receivers for Search and Rescue (SAR). GPS tracking is also especially useful for law enforcement.

GPS accuracy is affected by atmospherics, city buildings reflecting the signal, and the receiver's capability—none has a clock as accurate as the satellite's. The most accurate receivers, like those of the US Coast Guard, positioned to within 4 inches (10 cm).

Antenna array

GALILEO

NAVSTAR is maintained by the US Air Force 50th Space Wing from its headquarters in Schriever Air Force Base, Colorado.

European countries are developing their own Global Navigation Satellite System (GNSS)— Galileo, featuring enhanced SAR functions. Russia and China also have their own GPS satellites, GLONASS and COMPASS (BeiDou 2).

All **GPS satellites** have multiple **ATOMIC CLOCKS** that **LOSE** or **GAIN** just **one second** over **ONE MILLION** years.

EARTH IMAGING

During early crewed space missions, astronauts remarked on the surprising amount of detail they could see on Earth's surface. This led NASA to develop dedicated Earth imaging satellites.

The 1972 Earth Resources Technology Satellite (ERTS) (later renamed Landsat 1) was a Nimbus weather satellite equipped with a special video camera and a cutting-edge (for its time) multispectral scanner.

GLOBAL SURVEYORS

The USA's *Landsat* program has been using satellites to take pictures of Earth's surface continuously for the last 40 years. Landsats fly 560 miles (912 km) up on a Sun-synchronous, Polar orbit. The altitude is high enough for a global view, but low enough to show humankind's impact on the environment. The photographs are stunning. But the valuable data is from multispectral scanners. These record invisible wavelengths of light like infrared and ultraviolet, revealing hidden details. *Landsat* is used in farming, map-making, forestry, urban planning, climate effects, and mineral exploration.

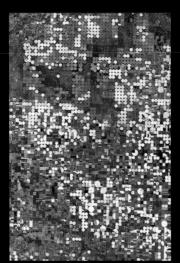

Circular irrigation farms in Kansas, USA create a bizarre abstract tapestry in this image from Landsat 7.

LANDSAT 8

1. **THERMAL INFRARED SENSOR** Creates "heat map"
2. **OPERATIONAL LAND IMAGER** Four-mirror telescope with multi-spectral scanner
3. **BOOSTER ROCKET**
4. **REACTION WHEEL**

Star tracker

Solar power panel

LANDSATS 7 and **8** complete over **14 orbits** per day, **covering** the **ENTIRE EARTH** every **16 DAYS.**

> *"If I had to pick one spacecraft development to save the world, I would pick ERTS and the satellites which will follow."* — Dr James Fletcher, NASA, 1975

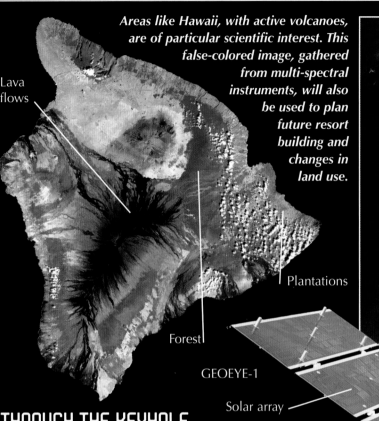

Areas like Hawaii, with active volcanoes, are of particular scientific interest. This false-colored image, gathered from multi-spectral instruments, will also be used to plan future resort building and changes in land use.

Lava flows

Plantations

Forest

GEOEYE-1

Solar array

Precious, unspoilt areas of the globe, like Mergui Archipelago on the coast of Myanmar (imaged by Landsat 5), are monitored for threats to their ecosystems by human development.

Reaction wheel

THROUGH THE KEYHOLE

Nations can use land imaging satellites for spying. US spy satellites were designated *KH*, or *KeyHole*, and until the 1980s had photographic film. Used film canisters would separate from the camera "ship" and re-enter Earth's atmosphere, floating down on parachutes to be snatched in mid-air by aircraft.

At least four *KH12* satellites are still active and may have formed the basis for the Hubble Space Telescope. Technical details of current government spy satellites remain classified.

Commercially operated satellite GeoEye-1 has its highest-detail images reserved for the US government. Other users include Google Maps.

Camera

Data downlink antenna

The USA's KH-9 "Big Bird" spy satellite (left), declassified in 2011, had a mapping camera and two panoramic cameras for stereo (3D) images. Its four detachable film capsules were equipped with booster rockets for re-entry. Technicians spooled film into them (right) before launch.

WEATHER SATELLITES

Modern-day meteorological satellites have made short-range weather forecasting highly accurate. From heat waves to hurricanes, weather satellites provide plenty of warning.

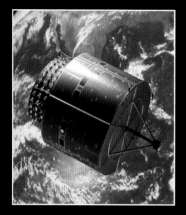

Synchronous Meteorological Satellite 1 *was the first weather sensor placed in geostationary orbit.*

GOES-R

1. **ADVANCED BASELINE IMAGER** Views Earth with 16 different spectral bands compared to five bands of previous *GOES*
2. **LIGHTNING MAPPER**
3. **EXTREME ULTRAVIOLET AND X-RAY SENSORS**
4. **SOLAR ULTRAVIOLET IMAGER**

BULLETIN BOARD

The animated satellite images seen on TV weather reports come from a fleet of three active satellites hovering over the American continent. These advanced *Geostationary Operational Environmental Satellites* (*GOES*) are run by the National Oceanic and Atmospheric Administration (NOAA).

GOES has several main instruments. A multichannel imager looks at infrared energy and reflected sunlight in the atmosphere. A sounder gathers vertical data for temperature and moisture, as well as ozone density. *GOES* can also monitor "space weather," like solar flares and magnetic storms.

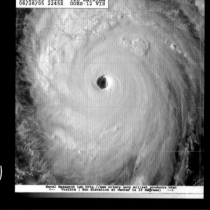

In 2005 GOES *satellite images of Hurricane Katrina provided hour-by-hour updates on an unfolding weather disaster.*

The **latest** fleet of **GOES**, cost **$10.9 BILLION** and begins launching in **2015**.

The versatile GOES-R is the next generation of weather satellites, gathering three times more information, in four times more detail, five times faster. In addition to weather, GOES-R will closely monitor aerosols, air quality, fires, and volcanic ash plumes.

1

2

Antenna array

Magnetometer (hidden)

3

4

Solar array

HURRICANE ANDREW
24 AUG 1992

This infrared image of Hurricane Andrew making landfall on the tip of Florida was taken by weather satellite GOES 7 in 1992. Twenty years ago, hurricane forecasts were issued just three days ahead of landfall. Now they are available five-plus days in advance due to more numerous satellites and more powerful computer models.

NOAA 19

1. **THERMAL VENTS**
2. **HIRS** High Resolution Infrared Radiation Sounder
3. **AVHRR** Advanced Very High Re... Radiometer—the main imager
4. **SENSOR SUITE** Assorted so... space weather detectors, and data colle...
5. **BATTERY PACK** One of six

Sun shade

Solar array

NOAA's POES polar weather satellites orbit at 541 miles (870km) in opposite directions. This ensures every spot on Earth is observed at least twice every 12 hours.

SAR antenna

SEEING THE WHOLE

While GOES scans the western half of the globe, other satellites complete the whole picture. NOAA's constellation of *Polar Operational Environmental Satellites* (*POES*) swing up and down around the Poles. They provide data to make long-range forecasts and climate predictions for shipping, aviation, farming, and the energy industries.

POES equipment includes a transponder to receive and retransmit SAR (Search And Rescue) beacon signals. It also gathers scientific data from ocean buoys and weather balloons.

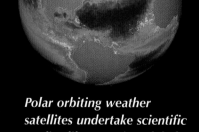

Polar orbiting weather satellites undertake scientific studies like mapping global patterns of sea plankton.

Countries without their own sophisticated weather radar rely on *POES* for their weather predictions and warnings.

RESEARCH SATELLITES

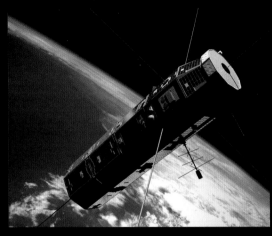

The Communications/Navigation Outage Forecasting System (C/NOFS) *is a US Air Force satellite for scanning Earth's ionosphere, where "twinkling" affects radio signals.*

NASA "A-TRAIN" CONSTELLATION

1. **GCOM-W1** Advanced microwave-scanning radiometer
2. **AQUA** Atmospheric infrared sounder, advanced microwave scanning radiometer, advanced microwave sounding unit, radiant imager, humidity sounder, spectro-radiometer
3. **CLOUDSAT** Cloud-profiling radar
4. **CALIPSO** Cloud-aerosol laser radar, imaging infrared radiometer, wide-field camera
5. **AURA** Infrared limb-scanning radiometer, microwave sounder, ozone monitor, tropospheric emission spectrometer

Recent cuts in space budgets coincided with rising concern about global warming. NASA's planetary experts were tasked with examining Earth's climate systems for some firm answers.

REMOTE SENSORS

NASA's Earth Observing System began in 1999 with the launch of multinational satellite *Terra.* Loaded with various kinds of spectral analyzers, *Terra* gathered information on ozone—which shields Earth from the Sun's ultraviolet rays—and pollution. *Aqua* (2002) studies rainfall and evaporation using instruments similar to weather satellites. *Aura* (2004) scans atmospheric layers and air quality. *Aqua* and *Aura* orbit with others in a close-spaced constellation, the A-Train, building high-definition 3D images of Earth's surface and atmosphere.

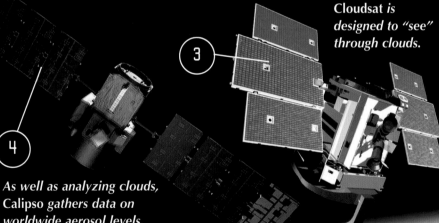

Cloudsat is designed to "see" through clouds.

As well as analyzing clouds, Calipso gathers data on worldwide aerosol levels.

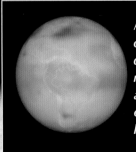

Aura's data on carbon dioxide levels, mapped onto a globe, show emission hotspots.

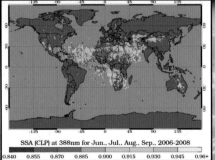

SSA (CLP) at 388nm for Jun., Jul., Aug., Sep., 2006-2008

0.840 0.855 0.870 0.885 0.900 0.915 0.930 0.945 0.96+

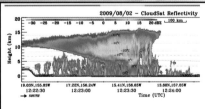

2009/08/02 - CloudSat Reflectivity

Cloudsat can show a section through an entire storm system.

NASA's polar-orbiting, remote sensing satellites enable scientists to monitor the ozone hole that appears every winter over the Antarctic.

ESA's Gravity Field and Steady-State Ocean Circulation Explorer (GOCE) had fins to help it glide through the wispy air 160 miles (260 km) high.

CLIMATE QUEST

Worldwide information on the chemical makeup of the atmosphere, changes in polar ice sheets, and water and carbon cycles are combined to produce long-term climate predictions. Science accepts that over the next few centuries, our planet will get hotter. But much remains mysterious. Further satellite launches should fill some gaps.

NASA's *Orbiting Carbon Observatory* (*OCO*), part of the A-train, will make the most detailed measurements yet of global carbon dioxide and other greenhouse gas levels.

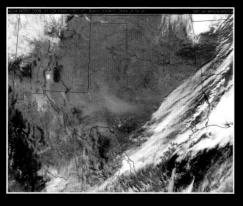

Aqua's spectro-radiometer is ideal for observing exceptional Earth events like wildfires or this west Texas dust storm.

Advanced microwave scanning radiometer

1

Aqua's primary mission is to observe the water cycle.

2

The A-train (afternoon train) crosses the Equator at 1:30 pm each day. It is led by GCOM-W1, whose mission extends Aqua's.

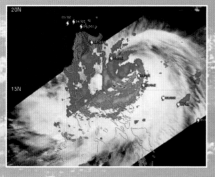

Aqua's rainfall-measuring instruments can detail the quantities of water inside a tropical storm.

The **FORECAST** for the **next 90 YEARS** is generally **WET** with **DRIER places** becoming more **ARID** and **WETTER places** getting **SWAMPED**.

The concept of orbiting telescopes was first suggested by astronomer Lyman Spitzer in 1949. As satellite technology matured, his precious dream slowly—but painfully—became reality.

From 1966 NASA operated two Orbiting Astronomical Observatory (OAO) satellites. These used ultraviolet and X-ray detectors to make exciting discoveries that spurred development of Hubble.

LIFTING THE VEIL

Spitzer lived to see his telescope built.

Work began on the first dedicated space telescope in 1977. Small enough to fit in the bay of a Space Shuttle, its 7.8-foot (2.4-meter) main mirror was small compared to the biggest Earth telescopes with 30-foot-plus (9-meter-plus) monsters. Unlike them it would reflect full-spectrum, undistorted starlight. Through its main and secondary mirrors, the light is directed into one of five instrument bays: a wide-field and planetary camera, a telephoto camera, two spectrographs, and a photometer (to measure brightness). After many setbacks the telescope, named after US astronomer Edwin Hubble—who discovered the Universe was expanding—was launched in 1990.

Hubble's big mirror had to perform flawlessly in microgravity. Grinding and polishing it to shape was a long and troublesome process that caused delays.

Discovery blasts off on Shuttle mission STS-31 with Hubble safely in its belly. The original launch date in 1986 was postponed when all Shuttles were grounded after the Challenger disaster.

Discovery's robo Canadarm placed the new telescope into orbit, 380 miles (611 km) above Earth. It was a scene destined to be repeated. Hubble was specifically designed for in-orbit repair — which would prove vital.

When Hubble went live, astronomers were horrified to find its images blurry. Hubble's mirror had been ground to the wrong shape! NASA was forced to design adjustment optics to fit in one of the instrument bays. The 1993 Shuttle servicing mission responsible also took an improved replacement camera, new solar panels, and pointing gyros.

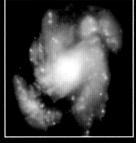

Before (above) and after (below): the improvement to Hubble's view was spectacular.

SHUTTLE ENDEAVOUR

WIDE-FIELD AND PLANETARY CAMERA 2

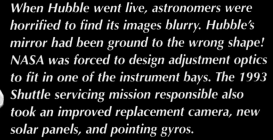

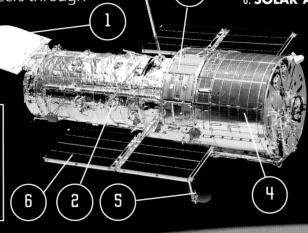

All telescope functions are controlled via satellite from Hubble Control at Goddard Space Flight Center near Washington, D.C.

CONTINUOUS SERVICE

Five servicing missions between 1993 and 2009 repaired and updated the telescope's spacecraft components and replaced its instruments. Today Hubble has the Wide-Field Camera 3 which images our Solar System and far distant objects. The Cosmic Origins Spectrograph analyzes ultraviolet light for the study of galaxy evolution. The Advanced Camera for Surveys views the Universe and planet-hunts. An infrared heat sensor, NICMOS, peers through interstellar gas, and the STIS spectrograph locates black holes.

The **HST cost** about **100** times **more** to **BUILD** and **maintain** than a typical **EARTH-BASED telescope.**

HUBBLE SPACE TELESCOPE

1. **APERTURE DOOR** Micrometeoroid shield
2. **SECONDARY MIRROR HOUSING**
3. **PRIMARY MIRROR HOUSING**
4. **INSTRUMENT MODULE**
5. **RADIO ANTENNAE** Two high-gain moveable antennae (narrow directional signals)
6. **SOLAR ARRAY** Replaced three times

Hubble in its final configuration was snapped by the departing Space Shuttle Atlantis *in 2009. All Low Earth Orbit satellites lose altitude over time. As Hubble has no engines, it had to be boosted back up during each service.*

HUBBLE'S EYE

A dying star's nebula as imaged by Hubble.

Since 1990, Hubble has taken over half a million images of the Cosmos. Its most famous pictures make world news and stimulate renewed public interest in astronomy, astrophysics, and cosmology.

EYE OF THE BEHOLDER

Fine guidance sensors are used to target an area on which all of Hubble's imagers are then trained. The imagers take three identical grayscale (shades of gray) pictures using carefully selected red, green, and blue filters. Using grayscale sensors allows Hubble to capture the maximum amount of detail. The three raw images are downloaded to Earth, assigned colors in a computer, and combined to create the final view. Objects like nebulae, which appear very faint (even to a passing spacecraft) are filtered and enhanced to show different chemical elements.

Starting in 1995, Hubble was occasionally trained on a small area of starless sky to take a series of days-long exposures. When processed, these "deep fields" revealed compact, faint galaxies hidden in the blackness. Their light has taken over nine billion years to reach us, showing them as they existed four billion years after the Universe began.

The Carina Nebula is a spectacular star-forming region, and fairly close at 6,500 light-years away. This image in natural color would be dark pinky-red (the optical color of ionized, or electrified, hydrogen). But, like most Hubble images, it has been computer-enhanced.

In 1994, Hubble watched Jupiter being hit by a series of comet fragments as Shoemaker-Levy 9 was pulled toward the giant planet. Each explosion represented the equivalent of detonating all atomic weapons on Earth at once.

HUBBLE'S LEGACY

As a scientific instrument, Hubble is a triumph. The telescope has enabled scientists to calculate the age of the Universe as 13.7 billion years. It has confirmed supermassive black holes at the centers of most galaxies; proven that quasars (the most powerful objects in the Universe) lie at the heart of young galaxies; made the first spectral analysis of a planet in another solar system; and shown nebulae from dying stars in unprecedented detail. Astronauts' spacewalks servicing Hubble even made the International Space Station a feasible project.

If **you** had **HUBBLE'S eye** you would be able to **SEE two fireflies** an **ARM'S LENGTH** apart from **2,568 MILES (4,133 KM)** away.

The Shuttle's last service, STS-125, ensured Hubble's operation to beyond 2014. It also installed a catchment ring on the rear shroud. This will enable a future spacecraft to safely "deorbit" Hubble when it finally loses power.

Soft-capture and rendezvous ring

This detailed study shows Galaxy NGC 2841, a spiral galaxy 46 million light years away. To compose it, Hubble's Wide-Field Camera 3 took four different filtered images, ranging from ultraviolet light, through visible to near-infrared.

INTERSTELLAR LOOKERS

Hubble was the first of NASA's Great Observatories—a four-satellite mission to collect cosmological data from all parts of the spectrum.

FAST PARTICLES

Visible light makes up only a very small part of the EM (electromagnetic) spectrum. Earth's atmosphere blocks other higher-energy EM radiation, like gamma rays, X-rays, and ultraviolet light. It also absorbs much of the lower-energy infrared rays.

Gamma rays are so energetic they pass through most materials and cannot be focused by mirrors. NASA's Compton Gamma Ray Observatory used sets of stacked detectors to measure them. Likewise, the third observatory, Chandra— launched in 1999—uses layers of curved mirrors to deflect fast-moving X-ray particles onto a detector. X-rays are produced as stars form, material is crushed inside black holes, and by dense objects like neutron stars.

The Compton Gamma Ray Observatory was launched in 1991 to look for the highest-energy particles in space. Gamma rays can indicate supernovae, black holes, pulsars, and quasars. CGRO was deliberately deorbited in 2000 after one of its gyroscopes failed.

Gamma ray burst detectors

Gamma ray detectors of various wavelengths

Solar array

CHANDRA X-RAY OBSERVATORY

1. **HIGH RESOLUTION MIRROR ASSEMBLY** Four pairs of nested mirrors
2. **ASPECT CAMERA**
3. **IMAGING SPECTROMETER** Accurately measures the energy of single photons
4. **HIGH RESOLUTION CAMERA**
5. **SPACECRAFT MODULE**

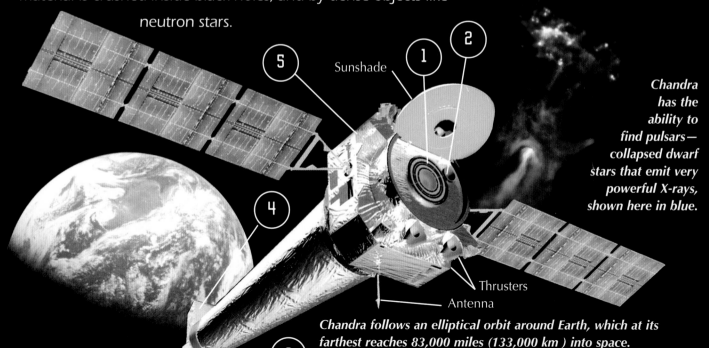

5

Sunshade

1

2

4

Chandra has the ability to find pulsars—collapsed dwarf stars that emit very powerful X-rays, shown here in blue.

Thrusters

Antenna

Chandra follows an elliptical orbit around Earth, which at its farthest reaches 83,000 miles (133,000 km) into space.

A supernova remnant in our Galaxy, called Kepler's Star, was imaged by Hubble using visible light (right). When this is combined with gamma ray, X-ray, and infrared information (far right), a large bubble of energy is revealed around the nebula.

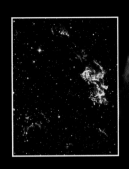

THE COOL COSMOS

All objects have a temperature and emit waves of light. Red light is the coolest visible temperature. Beyond red, getting colder, is infrared light—near, mid, and far. Cold objects in space, like dust clouds, are only visible with infrared instruments. Observing the infrared allows astronomers to see farther and in more detail. This is the main task of Hubble's successor, the infrared James Webb Space Telescope. From 2018 it will spend 10 years charting the history of the Universe, using a near-infrared camera and spectrometer, and mid-infrared instruments.

Webb will observe infrared radiation to capture fine detail, similar to how Spitzer sees objects like the Helix Nebula (below).

The fourth Great Observatory was the Spitzer Space Telescope, sent aloft in 2003. Spitzer was designed to see in the mid- to far-infrared. But as its coolant was exhausted, it was adjusted to near-infrared only.

JAMES WEBB SPACE TELESCOPE

1. PRIMARY MIRROR 18 gold-coated beryllium hexagons, total 21 feet (6.5 meters), unfolded in space

2. SECONDARY MIRROR

3. INSTRUMENT BAYS Housed behind mirror

4. SPACECRAFT BUS Control systems

5. SUN SHIELD Five thin layers of heat-resistant Kapton; outer layer coated with silicon

The JWST will orbit beyond the Moon, about 1 million miles (1.5 million km) from us, with the Sun and Earth at its back.

Sun/Earth facing

> JWST's most **SENSITIVE instruments** will be kept at **–447 ºF (–266 ºC)** until their **COOLANT** runs **OUT.**

SATELLITE ORBITS

Satellites orbit in ways that serve their function. Comsats are synchronized above a spot on Earth, while global research satellites loop around the Poles.

POPULAR EARTH ORBITS

1. **GEOSYNCHRONOUS (GSO)/GEOSTATIONARY (GEO)** Always 22,236 miles (35,786 km); GSO moves in a small figure-of-eight
2. **MOLNIYA ORBIT** Elliptical Russian comsat orbit
3. **MEDIUM EARTH ORBIT (MEO)** GPS satellite constellations
4. **SUN-SYNCHRONOUS POLAR ORBIT** Infrared satellites
5. **LOW EARTH ORBIT (LEO)** Scientific satellites

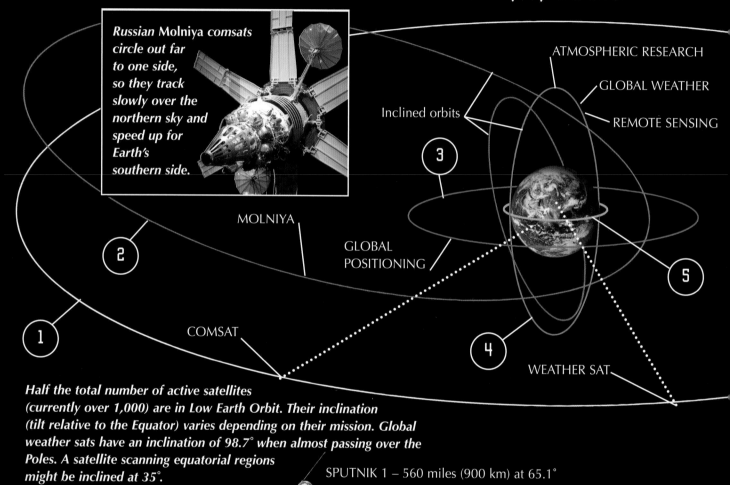

Russian Molniya comsats circle out far to one side, so they track slowly over the northern sky and speed up for Earth's southern side.

ATMOSPHERIC RESEARCH

GLOBAL WEATHER

REMOTE SENSING

Inclined orbits

3

MOLNIYA

2

GLOBAL POSITIONING

5

1

COMSAT

4

WEATHER SAT

Half the total number of active satellites (currently over 1,000) are in Low Earth Orbit. Their inclination (tilt relative to the Equator) varies depending on their mission. Global weather sats have an inclination of 98.7° when almost passing over the Poles. A satellite scanning equatorial regions might be inclined at 35°.

SPUTNIK 1 – 560 miles (900 km) at 65.1°

IRIDIUM – 485 miles (781 km) at 86.4°

LANDSAT 7 – 438 miles (705 km) at 98.2°

HUBBLE – 257 miles (414 km) at 28.5°

GOCE – 139 miles (224 km) at 96.7°

PATHWAYS FOR PEACE

KEEPING STATION

Satellites use spinning reaction wheels to adjust their attitude (orientation).

A satellite's orbital speed depends on how far it is from Earth's center—that is, the pull of Earth's gravity. GSO/GEO speed is about 6,870 miles (11,060 km) per hour. LEO speed averages 17,000 miles (27,360 km) per hour. Speeds are affected by Earth's imperfect shape (it bulges at the Equator), and the added pull of the Sun, Moon, and even Jupiter. LEO satellites also experience atmospheric drag.

Some satellites have onboard rockets or thrusters to reboost their altitude. When solar activity thickens Earth's high atmosphere, LEO satellites may need three altitude burns per week rather than three per year. This reduces their fuel and so their lifespan.

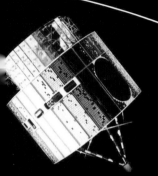

The latest geostationary satellites use very efficient plasma thrusters to maintain their altitude.

The stable orbit of geostationary satellites means they may be "repurposed." Retired from weather duties in 1989, GOES 3 is now a comsat.

FENGYUN SATELLITE

Satellites can be destroyed in orbit by Earth-based missiles. In 2007 China blew up an old FengYun weather satellite, creating the single largest debris field ever recorded in space.

SPACE JUNK

Satellites also burn fuel being moved to avoid collisions. Since 1957 more than 3,000 objects have been put into orbit. Two-thirds of them are defunct satellites, spent rocket stages, and other sizeable debris. Space junk travels at hypersonic speeds and any collision creates ever more particles. Currently, the US Space Surveillance Network tracks more than 18,000 orbital objects 4 inches (10 cm) and bigger. And 900 new satellites are estimated to join the crowd by 2020!

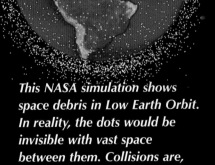

This NASA simulation shows space debris in Low Earth Orbit. In reality, the dots would be invisible with vast space between them. Collisions are, thankfully, very rare.

Future satellites in LEO may collect space debris and blast it into deep space.

For the **last 50 YEARS**, space **DEBRIS** has been **FALLING** to **Earth** at an **AVERAGE rate** of about **ONE** object **per DAY**.

FUTURE SATELLITES

The future of satellites ranges from swarms of tiny "nanosats" to gargantuan space elevators anchored by captured asteroids, and even satellite-versus-satellite space weaponry.

LEVERAGING ORBIT

The need for powerful launch rockets to send craft beyond Earth's atmosphere makes space exploration enormously expensive and dangerous. It might be easier to anchor a strong cable to an island and extend it, past even geostationary orbit, to 62,000 miles (100,000 km) out, then attach a captured asteroid as a counterweight to keep it taut. Such a tether could then carry laser-propelled platforms—space elevators—to lift material into orbit and back down again. The recent

This NASA concept depicts a space elevator in action. It could reduce costs of individual spaceflights by nine-tenths.

development of thin, amazingly strong carbon nanotubes brings the science fiction of these space elevators a little closer.

The vacuum of space would be perfect for laser weapons. Currently, the most effective weapons-grade lasers shoot a beam of infrared light—a wavelength that is absorbed by Earth's atmosphere.

In the 1980s, the US considered building a satellite defense platform with weapons to destroy incoming Soviet missiles. In response to this Strategic Defense Initiative (SDI), the Soviets attempted a prototype space-based laser that could bring down an SDI satellite. Thankfully both plans were shelved. So far, space has remained peaceful.

Future satellites could well become more autonomous, or robotic. During the Orbital Express mission in 2007, the US Defense Advanced Research Projects Agency (DARPA) used ASTRO, the Autonomous Space Transport Robotic Operations satellite, to dock with a prototype future satellite, NEXTSat. ASTRO transferred fuel and equipment to NEXTSat, all without human help.

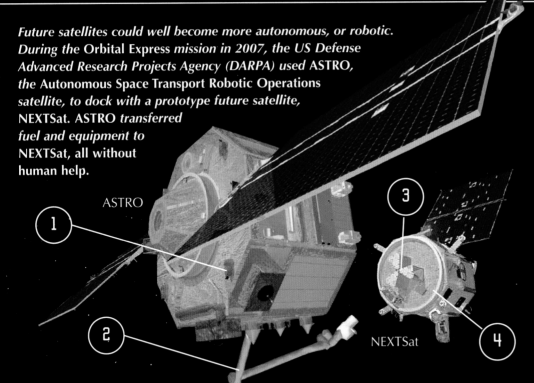

ASTRO

NEXTSat

ORBITAL EXPRESS

1. **THRUSTER**
2. **MANIPULATOR ARM**
Fitted with clamp and camera
3. **CAPTURE SYSTEM**
4. **SEPARATION RING**

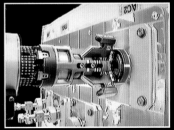

NASA used a robot arm to access and refuel old satellites that were never designed to be serviced, extending their lives.

DOD RINGS

1. **RINGS** Resonant Inductive Near-field Generation System
2. **SPHERES** Synchronized Position Hold Engage and Reorient robotic mini-satellite
3. **CONNECTING STRUTS**

Power pack

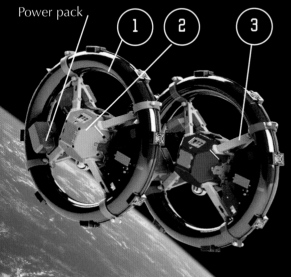

SATELLITE HELPERS

NASA plans robot-servicing satellites that could reach GEO and refuel many older communications and weather satellites. Mini-, micro-, and nanosatellites might fly in formation to inspect larger satellites or set up inexpensive radio- or remote-sensing constellations. For satellites too small to house thrusters, the US Department of Defense (DOD) has experimental RINGS satellites that generate electromagnetic fields to exchange power and fly in formation. Ever-increasing roles for satellites mean their future looks very bright indeed.

One day satellites could collect solar energy to beam down to Earth for power. The challenges are making mirrors light enough to launch and aiming the powerful microwave or laser beam accurately from GEO to a small collecting station.

The **SMALLEST** satellites are called **FEMTO-SATELLITES**, and are **about** the **SIZE** of a **large POSTAGE STAMP**.

TECH FILES – SATELLITE STATS

TYPE OF SATELLITE	OPERATIONAL	ORBIT	OPERATOR	APPLICATIONS	UNIT COST $
COMSATS					
BROADCASTING	More than 400	LEO/GEO/ MOL CONST	Intelsat, Pan Am Sat, and many more worldwide	Television/radio broadcast, radio communications, Internet/plus services	2–6 million + 50 million launch costs
TELEPHONE	More than 60	LEO/POL CONST	Iridium	Constant cellular phone coverage of entire Earth	5 million
MILITARY	6 (at least) 2 (so far)	GEO MEO/GEO	Milstar Global Broadcast Service	Secure, jam-resistant, worldwide Additional comms capability	800 million 300 million
GPS					
NAVIGATION	24-plus 24 10 (so far) 2 (so far)	MEO CONST	US Navstar (military and civilian), Russian GLONASS, Chinese BeiDou-2, EU Galileo	Sat-nav devices, tracking, mapping, Search And Rescue (SAR), satellite-guided weapons (smart bombs), geodesy, spaceflight	5.6 billion set up, plus 750 million each year (Navstar)
REMOTE SENSING					
EARTH IMAGING	2 5 More than 27	POL/LEO POL/LEO POL/LEO	US Geological Survey (Landsats 7 & 8) GeoEye/DigitalGlobe (WorldViews -1 & -2, Quickbird, GeoEye 1, etc) Other operators	Farm, forest, and range resources, mapping, geology, hydrology, coastal, environmental monitoring Digital maps, planning, multispectral imaging, spying, disaster monitoring As above Forecasting, nowcasting, SAR	800 million to 1 billion each 500 million average
WEATHER	3 2 More than 16	GEO/MEO POL/LEO	NOAA-GOES NOAA-POES Other weather sats	Global weather environment, SAR As above Climate, sea levels, pollution level	7 billion (next gen) 425 million
RESEARCH	More than 20 (NASA EOS only)	POL/LEO CONST	NASA Earth Observing System—Terra, Aqua, Aura, Cloudsat, etc.	cloud structure, atmosphere dynamics, global warming	30 million (ACRIMSAT) to 1 billion (Terra)
SPACE OBSERVING	17	LEO/MEO/ HEO	NASA: Hubble, Chandra, Spitzer, Fermi, Swift GRB, NuSTAR, IRIS, WISE, etc. ESA: Hubble, INTEGRAL, XMM Newton, Gaia, etc. JAXXA and others: ASTRO-EZ, SPRINT A, MOST, AGILE, ODIN	Observation and imaging with gamma rays, X-rays, ultraviolet, visible spectrum, infrared (near, medium, and far), submillimeter light, microwaves, radio waves, particle detection	2.5 billion (Hubble) 1.65 billion (Chandra), 880 million (Gaia) 720 million (Spitzer) 170 million (NuSTAR)

EO= Low Earth Orbit   MEO= Medium Earth Orbit   HEO=High Earth Orbit   POL= Polar Orbit   MOL=Molniya Orbit   GEO= Geostationary Orbit   CONST= Constellation

GLOSSARY

ASTEROID relatively small, rocky, or metallic space object orbiting the Sun; most are between 33 feet (10 m) and 620 miles (1,000 km) across

ATMOSPHERE layer of gases around a space object such as a planet

ATTITUDE position of a spacecraft or satellite; for example, its angle in relation to Earth or pointing at a star

COMET relatively small space object following a long, lop-sided orbit around the Sun that warms and glows when near the Sun

ELLIPTICAL oval-shaped, as for the orbits of many planets, spacecraft, and satellites

GRAVITY force of attraction between objects, which is especially huge for massive objects like planets and stars

MASS amount of matter in an object, in the form of numbers and kinds of atoms

MICROGRAVITY where the force of gravity from a nearby object, like a planet, is extremely weak or almost zero

MOON space object that orbits a planet. The single moon of Earth is usually known as the Moon (capital letter M)

ORBIT regular path of one object around a larger one, determined by the speed, mass, and gravity of the objects

PLANET large space object that has a spherical shape due to its gravity, and has cleared a regular orbital path around a star

RADIOMETER device that measures the strength or power of rays or radiation, such as radio waves, light waves, and X-rays

REENTRY returning from space to an object such as a planet, when friction with the thickening atmosphere slows the spacecraft but also causes immense heat

SATELLITE space object that orbits another, including man-made satellites and natural satellites like the Moon orbiting Earth or Earth orbiting the Sun

SPECTROMETER device that analyzes the range or spectrum of energy at different wavelengths, for example, the "rainbow" spectrum of visible light

INDEX